W9-BSC-565

PARANORMAL
INVESTIGATIONS

The Hope Diamond, Cursed Objects,

and Unexplained Artifacts

Andrew Coddington

Cavendish
Square

New York

Library of Congress Cataloging-in-Publication Data

Names: Coddington, Andrew.
Title: The Hope diamond, cursed objects, and unexplained artifacts / Andrew Coddington.
Description: New York : Cavendish Square, 2018. | Series: Paranormal investigations | Includes index.
Identifiers: ISBN 9781502628510 (library bound) | ISBN 9781502628527 (ebook)
Subjects: LCSH: Blessing and cursing--Juvenile literature. | Parapsychology--Juvenile literature.
Classification: LCC BF1558.C634 2018 | DDC 133.4'4--dc23

Editorial Director: David McNamara
Editor: Kristen Susienka
Copy Editor: Rebecca Rohan
Associate Art Director: Amy Greenan
Designer: Joseph Macri
Production Coordinator: Karol Szymczuk
Photo Research: J8 Media

Contents

Some believe that certain inanimate objects are full of evil energy.

INTRODUCTION

Curses

The world is an uncertain place. An ordinary life might be marked by several periods of misfortune: financial troubles, brushes with crime, the loss of a home, failing health, the death of a loved one. These tragedies are a part of life, but what if there were ordinary objects in the world that actually caused these misfortunes? What if there were places or things that radiate an evil energy that preys on people? For many around the world and throughout history, this is not just an idea—it is reality.

Nearly every culture has some belief in cursed objects, things that cause unnatural harm to the person who owns or uses them. Often, these objects have roots in a tragic past, and according to those who believe in **curses**, something from a tragedy sticks with the objects, becoming a part of them and spelling disaster for anyone who might come across them.

Almost anything can be a cursed object: a doll put under a spell by a murdered witch, a car owned by a movie star who died in a wreck, a burial ground protected by the power of misfortune. Even normally rational people may occasionally fall into a certain **superstition** to avoid bringing a curse down on themselves.

The origins of an object's rumored curse might lie in a long history of tragedy.

Despite this abundance of allegedly unfortunate objects, few come close to one of the most legendary of all: the Hope Diamond. The recorded history of this jinxed gem stretches back centuries, and over that time period, dozens of people have claimed ownership of this stunning stone—traveling merchants, French monarchs, gem collectors, and other wealthy elites. Of the owners of the Hope Diamond, a few have experienced such great catastrophes that many claim it to be cursed. Fortunes have been lost, kings executed, and entire countries thrown into chaos and war. The history of the Hope Diamond is certainly one of intrigue, but is it true that it, as well as other objects around the world, are sources of tragedy? It is time to investigate the curse.

LUCKY CHARMS

Just as there are objects that are believed to be cursed or unlucky, there is an abundance of objects that many trust to bring good luck to their owners. A sports fan may don a sun-bleached baseball cap or pull on a tattered, mustard-stained jersey the day of a big game, or a student may use a certain chewed-up pen or pencil for an exam. Someone may rub a certain stone before a job interview because they think these objects are responsible for their successes in the past.

Just like cursed objects, the practice of carrying a lucky object has roots in the beliefs of ancient peoples. Many cultures consider certain materials, such as salt and iron, naturally magical substances because of their purity. Ever wonder why people throw spilled salt over their shoulder or hang an iron horseshoe in their house? Both salt and iron, from which horseshoes used to be made, were once believed to ward off evil spirits. This leads many to believe that they are sources of good luck.

Horseshoes are thought to bring good luck.

Some legends about curses begin
with witches casting spells on
ordinary people and things.

CHAPTER ONE

The History of Cursed Objects

What distinguishes a cursed object from any regular object? As the name suggests, something that is cursed has been somehow infused with **supernatural** power that causes harm or misfortune to befall a person, people, or things. Also known as a hex or jinx, a curse is started when a person petitions some higher power, such as a god or spirit, through a wish, prayer, or spell, to cause harm or misfortune to those who behave in a certain way. For example, a person might curse a pencil (the object) with the condition that if a person uses it without asking (the cursed behavior), then the user will fail a test or paper (the misfortune).

Curses have been around for a long time, possibly longer than history itself. According to the creation story in the Bible, the first humans were victims of a curse placed on them by God. When God created the first people, Adam and Eve, he gave them an easy and bountiful life in the Garden of Eden. This comfortable arrangement was conditional on one thing, however: to avoid eating the fruit of the Tree of Knowledge. Adam and Eve eventually ate from the tree because they were influenced by an evil serpent. As a result, God cursed them. For Adam, the earth would no longer offer its bounty easily, and instead he would have to work tirelessly to grow his food. For Eve, her body itself, as well as those of all later women, would be cursed, subject to intense pain as a result of childbirth. As for the serpent, God made him the lowest of all creatures—a snake—doomed to slither on his belly.

As a result of their disobedience, the first people in the Biblical creation story were cursed and forced to leave Eden.

Taboo

Curses are very closely related to **taboos**. Taboos are a type of custom within a culture that forbids a certain behavior. This makes them similar to laws, but taboos are different because they are more concerned with making sure people behave morally, not just as good citizens in a community. For example, it is considered by many to be taboo to use swear words (also known as "curse words" or profanities), but there are not many laws that prohibit using them.

Many of the world's most legendary curses also involve one of civilizations' greatest taboos: disturbing the dead. Practically every culture has some belief in an afterlife, and it was common throughout history for the deceased—especially the noble or wealthy—to be buried with certain possessions that were thought to be of use in the next world. Archaeologists working around the world have discovered graves, tombs, and mounds filled with artifacts ranging from pottery and household items to weapons and even luxury items, such as fine furniture, gold jewelry, and precious gems. Untold troves of cultural (and financial) wealth still remain buried in the ground or sealed behind stone.

Many cultures throughout history believed that the belongings accompanying the dead would prove useful in the afterlife.

Archaeologists are not the only ones who have dug to find these valuable artifacts. Ever since humanity first started burying its dead with important objects, thieves and grave robbers have been disturbing the deceased to make off with easy pickings—after all, a dead man won't fight back if you steal his gold earrings, right?

Keeping Thieves at Bay

Societies have invented a couple ways to try to prevent these robbers from stealing from the deceased. One option is to make it difficult to access the wealth of the tomb through engineering. For example, the pyramid built for the Egyptian pharaoh Khufu, the oldest and largest of the three pyramids located at Giza, was built of stone blocks weighing between 2.5 to 15 tons (2.7 to 13.6 metric tons) each, and walls up to 262 feet (80 meters) thick. In addition to being a monumental testament to Khufu's power and greatness, the thick stone walls helped deter anyone who might try to burrow in. Moreover, the passages that led into the pyramid as well as the corridor to Khufu's funerary chamber were each designed to include grooves that would release massive granite blocks known as portcullises once construction was finished, thereby blocking the way into and out of a funeral chamber.

However, clever engineering could only work so well— after all, despite the sophisticated security system built into the Great Pyramid, archaeologists have managed to gain access to it. In order to prevent the honored dead from being robbed, many cultures believed the best strategy might be to deter a person from disturbing a tomb in the first place, and the best way to do so was to put a curse on it.

The general idea is that places of burial are protected by a spell; should anyone disturb any part of the tomb, be it the

William Shakespeare's grave in the Church of the Holy Trinity, Stratford-upon-Avon, England, is protected by a curse of the Bard's own design.

GOOD FRIEND FOR JESUS' SAKE FORBEAR,
TO DIG THE DUST ENCLOSED HERE.
BLESSED BE THE MAN THAT SPARES THESE STONES,
AND CURSED BE HE THAT MOVES MY BONES.

Shakespeare's Gravestone - Holy Trinity Stratford-upon-Avon

THE GRAVE
OF THE POET
WILLIAM
SHAKESPEARE
1564-1616

body or the riches buried there, that person would experience bad luck, serious injury or illness, or even death. The idea behind these curses was to make a superstitious robber question whether or not the short-term gain of wealth was worth risking his life over. Allegedly cursed tombs are common among two of the ancient world's greatest civilizations, the Egyptians and the Chinese.

This huge cairn at the top of Knocknarea outside Sligo, Ireland, is the final resting place of the ancient queen Maeve.

The idea of a protective curse on a burial ground has been popularized in films, such as Steven Spielberg's Indiana Jones series and horror movies, and in folklore. A common **trope** in American folklore and pop culture is the idea that Native American burial grounds are cursed. This concept has appeared in movies such as *Poltergeist* and even primetime television shows like NBC's *Parks and Recreation*. The general story goes that a person or family, usually of white European descent, desecrates a gravesite originally constructed by Native Americans by building on top of it. In many cases, the builders are told about the burial grounds by another party, such as a construction worker or archaeologist who finds artifacts, or a member of a Native American tribe, but they choose to proceed with the project anyway. In disturbing the remains, however, they become the targets of the curse: their house may be haunted by vengeful spirits of the dead or harassed by guardians from Native American folklore, or individuals may begin to suffer from bad luck. Eventually, the activity escalates to the point where the family is either forced to abandon their home or suffer even worse consequences.

The myth of cursed burial grounds has many different interpretations. For one, the legend is a manifestation of either the guilt or frustration among European colonizers who arrived in the New World and stamped out the Native cultures that already existed there. It may also be a way for those displaced and disenfranchised Native peoples to exact some sort of retribution on their oppressors. Additionally, it serves as a metaphor for the colonization of America itself: all land is a Native American burial ground for a dead or dying culture.

The Curse of the Pharaohs

Some of the most popular hotbeds of cursed gravesites are pyramids. Among them is the curse of King Tutankhamen's tomb.

On November 26, 1922, after months spent digging amid the sands of the Egyptian desert, British archaeologist Howard Carter made the discovery of the century: the lost tomb of King Tutankhamen. Inside, Carter, along with his sponsor Lord Carnarvon, discovered fabulous wealth that had been left undisturbed for three thousand years, including life-size gold statues of the ancient king and a solid gold sarcophagus encrusted with jewels.

Many feared that Carter had unleashed something far more sinister once he cracked the door to the tomb. The local

CURSED HORCRUXES

The idea of cursed objects has appeared in one of the most successful series of children's books in recent times, Harry Potter. In the fantastic world invented by author J.K. Rowling, Harry Potter must find and destroy a number of objects that have been cursed by the most powerful evil wizard, Lord Voldemort. These "horcruxes," as they are known, are ordinary objects that have been imbued with a shred of Voldemort's soul to act as a sort of insurance policy: should someone destroy Voldemort's body, horcruxes can resurrect him.

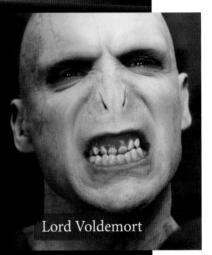

Lord Voldemort

In addition to being the product of dark magic, the horcruxes also seem to radiate evil. Like many supposed cursed objects in the real world, the horcruxes seem to have abilities that torment their owners. The horcruxes are intent on preserving themselves. For example, one of the first horcruxes takes the form of a diary owned by Voldemort during his school years (*Harry Potter and the Chamber of Secrets*). When this is placed in the hands of young Ginny Weasley, the diary begins communicating with her, putting her under a spell and instructing her on how to bring Voldemort back to life.

The horcruxes in Harry Potter are very powerful evil artifacts. As such, they require very powerful magic to destroy them, such as piercing with a fang from a giant poisonous basilisk or striking with the goblin-made sword of the legendary wizard Godric Gryffindor.

workmen Carter had hired refused to go any deeper into the tomb, believing further trespass would make them targets of an ancient curse. Undaunted, Carter and Lord Carnarvon carried on into the tomb and proceeded to catalog and remove its contents. While trying to remove the innermost sarcophagus, Carter's team accidentally beheaded the mummified king. Within months of the transgression, Lord Carnarvon died of blood poisoning, and five others who had been present at the opening of the tomb died over the course of the next decade.

British archaeologist Howard Carter opens the tomb of King Tut on November 26, 1922.

The succession of deaths associated with Carter's expedition led many newspapers to speculate that the archaeologist had brought an ancient curse down on his team when he disturbed King Tut's rest. The death of Lord Carnarvon and the others became the centerpiece of the so-called Curse of the Pharaohs.

In reality, the "curse" likely does not exist at all. Lord Carnarvon was widely known to suffer from bad health, and the area where the expedition had set up camp in the scorching Egyptian desert was unsanitary. All told, only six of the twenty-six people who had first excavated the tomb died within a decade, and Carter himself, who as expedition leader would have surely been squarely in the crosshairs of any such curse, died almost two decades after his discovery.

THE CURSE OF THE BAMBINO

Some of the most widely circulated rumors about curses involve sports. Many ordinary people become extremely superstitious when it comes to the outcomes of athletic competitions, and as a result, practically every major sport has its jinxes. Everything from players to teams to whole cities and even video games are believed to be cursed.

One of the longest-running curses in sports concerns baseball, a team, and arguably the greatest player to ever swing a bat. In 1920, the Boston Red Sox traded legendary hitter Babe Ruth to their rival, the New York Yankees. Ruth, also known as the "Great Bambino," was widely considered the most talented player at the time and helped the Red Sox earn three of its five World Series championships before being traded. The deal seemed to bring good luck to the Yankees. The new star not only set a new home run record while with the team but also helped them win their first championship in 1923—and three more after that, establishing the Yankees as one of baseball's top franchises.

As much as the Yankees benefitted from the trade, the Red Sox fell into a slump that lasted for decades. After Boston let go of the Bambino, the team failed to win a championship for the better part of a century, leading many to speculate (some seriously) that the Red Sox were the victims of the so-called "Curse of the Bambino." The "curse" lasted until 2004 when the Red Sox won their first title in eighty-four years. Since then, the Red Sox have won two more championships, in 2007 and 2013.

The Hope Diamond as it appears on display at the Smithsonian

Uncovering the Hope Diamond

The Hope Diamond is perhaps the most famous precious stone in the world for a number of reasons. For one thing, it is a unique, deep blue color, which places it among the rarest of colored diamonds in the world. For another, it is unusually large, weighing in at 45.52 **carats**, making it the largest **cut** blue diamond in the world. Its beauty and rarity has made it a centerpiece at the Smithsonian Museum of Natural History in Washington, DC, where it has been seen by over one hundred million visitors in the nearly six decades it has been on display. Experts estimate that the gem would fetch upwards of $250 million if the Smithsonian should ever sell it.

The allure of the Hope Diamond may not be the only thing that has garnered so much attention over the centuries. Since its discovery in India in the mid-seventeenth century, the Hope Diamond may be the source of a curse that has left certain owners penniless, homeless, or, in the most frightening of cases, dead.

The Geology of the Hope Diamond

The Hope Diamond, like other such naturally occurring gemstones, was formed deep in the earth more than a billion years ago. Diamonds are made up of pure carbon, which is among the most abundant elements in the universe. Carbon's tendency to form natural patterns, called polymers, as well as its ability to bond with atoms of other elements, makes it one of the fundamental building blocks of things ranging from fossil fuel sources, such as oil and coal, to plastics, diamonds, and even life itself.

Although this hole at a diamond mine in Russia may look deep, diamonds are actually formed many miles beneath Earth's surface.

An abundance of carbon has been buried deep in the earth over the course of billions of years. The carbon that eventually becomes diamonds is located in a part of the earth known as the **mantle**, a 1,802 mile- (2,900 kilometer-) thick center of Earth's interior. The mantle is located between 3 and 25 miles (8 and 32 km) below the surface of the Earth, also known as the **crust**, and amounts for 84 percent of Earth's total volume. Scientists aren't exactly sure where this carbon has come from, though it seems likely that it originated from two different sources. On the one hand, some carbon that was present during the formation of Earth some 4.6 billion years ago has stayed in the mantle. On the other hand, carbon can make its way into the mantle when things on Earth's surface with a lot of carbon, such as plants and animals, are buried in the ground. Over time, the movement of huge slabs of rock known as **tectonic plates** shift, causing them to crash into or overlap one another and sometimes driving one plate sideways and downward deep into the mantle and carrying these carbon deposits with them.

Unlike the relatively cool and solid crust of the earth, the mantle below is extremely hot and viscous. The temperature of the mantle varies, averaging 1,832 degrees Fahrenheit (1,000 degrees Celsius) near the crust to 6,692 °F (3,700 °C) near Earth's core. Much of the rock that makes up the mantle is molten and traverses through the mantle at approximately the speed of freshly poured asphalt. In addition to its high heat, the mantle is also defined by the extraordinary pressure at play there. At the top of the mantle nearest the core, the pressure averages 200,000 pounds per square inch (PSI), while nearer the core, pressures can exceed 20 million PSI. (By comparison, Earth's atmosphere only exerts about 14.7 PSI.)

This intense heat and pressure that is characteristic of the mantle affects the way carbon arranges itself. At approximately

WHAT CAUSES DIAMOND COLOR?

Colored, or "fancy," diamonds

When most people think of a diamond, they think of white, or "colorless," diamonds. These are among the most commonly used in jewelry, such as diamond earrings and engagement rings. Most mined diamonds have slightly yellow hues, which was caused by the presence of other elements during the formation of the stone. Many consumers, influenced by decades of commercial advertising, believe that these stones are less valuable because of these "impurities."

Certain diamonds, such as the Hope Diamond, however, are so vibrantly colored that the "impurity" of their composition is actually a selling point. Rich coloration is extremely rare in diamonds—even more so than pure white diamonds—making them much more highly sought after (and much more expensive) than most white diamonds. These stones are known as fancy diamonds and cover practically the entire color spectrum, from bright yellow and orange to fuzzy pink or vivid red, violet, or green, to even deep black.

Blue diamonds like the Hope Diamond are among the rarest in the world; the Smithsonian estimates that only one out of every two hundred thousand diamonds will have a blue tint, and even then most likely appearing a grayish or pale blue as opposed to the deep, sapphire-like blue of the Hope Diamond. Blue coloration is caused by the presence of boron in the diamond's formation—slight amounts of boron create a faint blue hue, and greater amounts give rise to the deep blue seen in the Hope Diamond. Interestingly, the world's most famous and precious diamond may in fact be less chemically "pure" than the white diamonds found on countless pieces of jewelry—ironic considering how diamonds are commonly marketed today.

100 miles (160 km) below Earth's surface, the heat and pressure of the mantle combine to cause carbon trapped there to begin arranging itself in regular geometric, or crystalline, form, thus creating a diamond. Just as a blacksmith uses the heat of a furnace and the pressure of hammer strikes to harden steel, diamonds are "forged" in the fire and forces at work within the earth itself, making them the hardest naturally occurring known substances in the world.

An Explosive Birth

The depth at which diamonds are formed is so deep and the pressure and heat so great that there is no way that people can dig down there. Even sophisticated drilling equipment using heat-resistant technology would either melt or be crushed well before they came close to reaching the mantle. So how is it that diamonds reach Earth's surface? The answer is something as equally powerful, elemental, and violent as the forces that create diamonds in the first place: volcanoes. The extreme heat in the mantle causes rocks to liquefy into magma. Magma is less dense than the rock surrounding it, so it naturally rises through the mantle, pooling in magma chambers underground. Superheated gases caught in these chambers exert enormous pressure, and once a crack or fissure in the roof of the chamber forms, the gas and magma pour out, sometimes explosively.

Only very powerful, very old volcanoes the likes of which have not been seen for some time are responsible for the fact that diamonds are found relatively close to Earth's surface. Long ago, when Earth was hotter than it is today, super violent volcanoes, whose magma originated at around the same depth that diamonds are formed, erupted, carrying diamonds with them. Once the volcanic material cooled,

Magma from ancient super volcanoes carried diamonds to Earth's surface.

the diamonds that were brought to the surface were buried there. That explains why many of the world's mined diamonds have been found in or around Kimberlite deposits, because Kimberlite is an **igneous** rock, meaning that it is formed from solidified magma or lava.

A Curse in the Making

When ancient humans first witnessed the unbridled eruption of volcanoes spewing black smog and raining fire, it's no wonder many imagined the space beneath Earth's surface to be the location of a violent and evil realm, inhabited by dark forces intent on spreading misery to humans above. Scientists have concluded that the only thing beneath our feet is mostly molten rock being moved around by powerful but understandable forces. Nevertheless, it is interesting that the same frightful explosions also carry with them diamonds, whose purity and properties to reflect and refract light has for centuries captured the desire of humankind. If the stories of the Hope Diamond's curse are to be believed, perhaps it is not a coincidence that the alluring gemstone originated in the same place once rumored to be the source of evil in the world.

Although the formation of diamonds is a fascinating process, there is nothing geologically unique about the Hope Diamond. True, its distinct blue coloration is rare among diamonds, but it is by no means the only blue diamond in the world, and there are many other diamonds similar in size and even larger. How, then, did the Hope Diamond earn the reputation of being cursed? The answer lies in a complicated story that stretches back nearly five centuries and involves both factual history as well as sensationalist reporting.

THE BIGGEST DIAMOND OF ALL

Contrary to popular belief, the Hope Diamond is not the largest in the world. That title belongs to a stone discovered in the Premier Mine in Pretoria, South Africa, in 1905. The gem, nicknamed the "Cullinan" after the mine's owner, Sir Thomas Cullinan, weighed 3,106 carats, or 1.33 pounds (0.6 kilograms). (By comparison, the Hope Diamond today weighs in at 45.52 carats, which made the Cullinan diamond at the time of its discovery over sixty-eight times larger.)

Cullinan sold the diamond to the provincial government in South Africa, which later gave it to the English king Edward VII on the monarch's birthday. Because Edward was worried the one-of-a-kind stone might be stolen, he arranged to have a decoy diamond protected by police be shipped at the same time as the Cullinan. The real stone, meanwhile, was packaged in an ordinary crate alongside other cargo.

The enormous Cullinan was later cut into over one hundred other stones by the renowned Dutch jeweler Joseph Asscher. The largest of these, called the Star of Africa I or Cullinan I, is 530 carats, making it the largest of its kind in the world. It was used as one of King Edward's **crown jewels** and, along with the second- and third-largest stones made from the Cullinan diamond, were used as crown jewels for the British monarchy. Today, the three are on display at the Tower of London in England.

The Hope Diamond, pictured here in 2010 in a temporary platinum setting, has captured the desire and imagination of countless people over the centuries.

CHAPTER THREE

Fates and Fortunes

The history of the stone that would later become known as the Hope Diamond begins in India. In the mid-seventeenth century, Baron Jean-Baptiste Tavernier, a French explorer and gem merchant, became the first European to acquire the Hope Diamond. In 1676, Tavernier published *Travels in India*. This book describes the Indian diamond mines as well as several gems that had come under his possession and which he later sold to the French king. Among these was a crudely cut, triangularly shaped, deep blue (so deep that Tavernier described it as being a "beautiful violet") stone weighing 112 $^3/_{16}$ carats (approximately the size of an adult man's fist). It came to be called the Tavernier Blue. The diamond did not become known as the Hope Diamond until 1839, when a gem collector by the name of Henry Thomas Hope came to possess it.

The Tavernier Blue

Tavernier's published accounts, such as the *Travels*, provides a wealth of information about his voyages, but unfortunately for historians, he has little to say about the details of his "acquisitions." Where the gems were unearthed, their owners,

Jean-Baptiste Tavernier

what they were used for, and the price Tavernier paid for them (or if he even paid for them at all) remains a mystery to this day. Always the businessman, Tavernier withheld this information, as it may have had a negative effect on the prices of his products when he returned to Europe.

It has been widely speculated that the Tavernier Blue was first excavated from Kollur Mine, located in the southeastern Indian state of Andhra Pradesh. The Kollur Mine has produced many of the world's largest and most famous diamonds, including the Koh-i-Noor, or "Mountain of Light," diamond. (Interestingly, the

Koh-i-Noor diamond bears many similarities to the Tavernier Blue: both were sold to European monarchy—the Koh-i-Noor was sold to British queen Victoria in the mid-nineteenth century—and both are also rumored to be cursed.)

The Curse Awakens

The vagueness of Tavernier's original account in *Travels in India*, combined with rumors of the stone's curse, later sparked rampant speculation about how the French merchant came by the stone in the first place. As the list of the diamond's owners who met bad ends grew over the centuries, a rumor was born that Tavernier may have acquired the gem through nefarious means.

The rumor quickly became one of the most often-told legends about the Hope Diamond in 1921, when author and movie director Henry Leyford Gates wrote *The Mystery of the Hope Diamond*. Despite the book's romantic language, it blurred the lines between fact and fiction, claiming that it was based on "the personal narrative of Lady Francis Hope." The account would establish one of the most enduring legends about Tavernier. Gates wrote that Tavernier actually stole the stone from a Hindu statue:

> That night, while the temple fires smoldered against the coming of dawn; and while priests and bayardes slept the exhaustion that both holiness and mischief bring, a solitary figure crept through the shadows and into the sacred circle at the base of the idol across which none but the high priest's feet had ever trod. When the ray of the moon had shifted so that the image was black in the shadows, a foreign, irreverent hand slid to its throat and rested there, shutting out for a second the glints of the great blue stone. When the hand came away, the glinting was gone.

The alleged theft and subsequent sale of the Hope Diamond brought Tavernier great wealth and prestige but also made him the target of a Hindu priest's curse. When Tavernier visited a French psychic, he warned the merchant, "Be upon your guard, my noble Baron! In the betrothal gem of Brisbun [the Hope Diamond] there is imprisoned Sita's curse for every hand that may profane it with irreverent touch!" Tavernier brushed the warning off, but his fate was sealed. According to Gates, karma caught up with Tavernier while he was camped outside of Moscow, Russia. There, a pack of dogs descended on his tent and "tore his body into countless shreds."

REVENGE OF THE HOPE DIAMOND! OR MAYBE NOT ...

Although Tavernier did die near Moscow in 1689, there is no historical evidence that he was mauled to death in a tent by dogs, as Gates suggests. According to gemologist Richard W. Wise, author of *The French Blue*, Tavernier, who was Protestant, had left his native France late in life to escape the growing religious persecution there. He eventually stopped in Russia and probably settled in a community of Moscow known as the Nemetskaya Sloboda, the "German Suburb," which was home to a number of Western European expatriates. The Russian czar Peter the Great, who was interested in Western European culture, was known to have visited the German suburb so often that, according to historian Robert K. Massie, "he seemed almost to live there." It seems probable that Tavernier, a well-traveled and accomplished Frenchman, enjoyed a degree of luxury before he died at the ripe old age of eighty-four.

Tavernier sold the famous diamond to King Louis XIV of France (pictured here).

The Crown Jewel

Since the rumors about the diamond's original owner's untimely death are largely romantic speculation, the history of the Hope Diamond as a cursed object begins in earnest in the seventeenth and eighteenth centuries, when it came into the possession of the French monarchy. The stone remained in the hands of either the French king or the government for over a century; during that time, its individual owners experienced a series of unfortunate fates, and the nation itself underwent one of the most brutal and bloodiest periods in world history.

The first "confirmed victim" of the Hope Diamond's curse is generally considered to be King Louis XIV, the so-called "Sun King." In 1668, the merchant Tavernier brought the large, rough diamond to France, where he sold it alongside a number of other gemstones to King Louis. The Tavernier Blue was cut by Jean Pittan, one of Louis's court jewelers, sometime between 1669 and 1673. The new stone weighed roughly 69 carats and was placed in a gold setting with a blue ribbon to be worn as a necklace. The diamond was then called the "Blue Diamond of the Crown," or simply the "French Blue." In the minds of many, the French Blue claimed Louis XIV as its first victim when, in 1715, the king died of gangrene, a disease caused by reduced blood supply to the tissues, which results in cell death. Also known as "trench foot" after the scores of World War I soldiers who came down with the disease, gangrene is typified by the spread of decaying, dark-green tissue, usually beginning in the extremities, such as the fingers or toes, and is generally accompanied by a strong stench of rotting flesh.

When Louis XIV died, his only surviving heir was a great-grandson, who became Louis XV. However, he was only five years old at the time, and many believed the boy king would not survive into adulthood. He did survive, though, and ended up leaving his own mark on the French Blue. He had the stone placed in a new setting, designed to be used as a ceremonial jewel in honor of the Catholic knightly order known as L'Ordre de la Toison d'Or, or Order of the Golden Fleece. Louis XV's reign proved problematic for France, bankrupting the nation through several wars with rival European nations and his

FIT FOR A KING

Although it was commonly believed that the French Blue was the precursor to the Hope Diamond, this theory was confirmed to be true only recently.

In 2009, Professor Francois Farges at the National d'Histoire Naturelle in Paris uncovered a lead replica of the French Blue dating back to the seventeenth century. (At the time, it was common for jewelers to make replicas of precious gems out of common metals, such as lead, while designing settings.) Using the Hope Diamond itself, Farges discovered that the stone from which the lead model was made must have been the same stone that was later recut into the Hope Diamond. Until that point, no one realized that the replica, which was shaped to resemble a rounded triangle, corresponded with the French Blue. Using a computer modeling program, French mineralogists discovered that the French Blue was very likely mounted against yellow gold and that its unique cut helped to reflect and refract the gold behind it in a starburst pattern, making the French Blue a fitting centerpiece for the so-called "Sun King's" crown.

The French Blue may have looked something like this prior to being stolen in 1792

court's lavishness. In 1774, at the age of sixty-four, Louis XV came down with smallpox. What began as a headache and fever gave way to blackened pustules, a signature symptom of the disease. He suffered for nearly a month, as the oozing pustules began to deform his face and choke him. He ultimately died on May 10.

Louis XV's successor was his twenty-year-old grandson, Louis XVI. King Louis XVI and his wife, Marie-Antoinette, are often synonymous with political disaster. Along with the wealth and prestige of the monarchy, the two inherited a desperate state of affairs: the number of wars commenced under Louis XIV and continued by Louis XV had made France the enemy of much of Europe. The decades of warfare, combined with the opulence of the monarchy, which was largely inflated by Louis XVI's predecessors, put a strain the finances of the country. To compensate, the king levied enormous taxes on the people, many of whom suffered as a result of food shortages.

Compounding the matter further, the French monarchy, as well as much of the noble class, had grown increasingly alienated from the people, with the king withdrawing deeper and deeper into the gilt rooms of Versailles Palace. Resentment for the ruling elites grew among the commoners during this time, bubbling over on July 14, 1789, when a mob captured the Bastille, a fortified prison in Paris, and took the city's governor hostage. One hundred civilians and eight guards died over the course of the fighting, and the governor and his officers were eventually beheaded and their heads paraded through the city on pikes. France was faced with a revolution.

Louis XVI, for his part, was an intelligent ruler with an aptitude for mechanics and engineering, as well as a background in political philosophy, and he was sympathetic to the plight of his nation's people. However, though he seemed to respect the movement to reform France's political and social structure, he wavered on many of its most important points, including ending the privileges given to the nobility and authorizing the *Déclaration des droits de l'homme et du citoyen*, the Declaration of the Rights of Man and the Citizen.

Louis XIV's irresolution earned him the ire of the revolutionaries. In 1789, the people arrested Louis XVI, Marie-Antoinette, and the rest of the royal family at Versailles and relocated them to Paris. After Louis and his family tried unsuccessfully to escape, Louis stood trial in 1792 and was found guilty of treason and crimes against the state. On January 21, 1793, heavy guards marched Louis XVI to the guillotine before a swell of revolutionaries. That morning, around 10:15 a.m., the last of the French kings was beheaded. His wife, Marie-Antoinette, was not far behind. In October of the same year, she met the same fate as her husband.

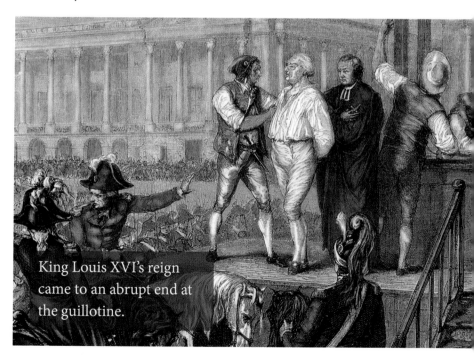

King Louis XVI's reign came to an abrupt end at the guillotine.

In September 1792, a week of looting broke out in Paris as a result of the chaos of the French Revolution. During this time, the French Blue was stolen, disappearing from history for two decades. Its departure from the French monarchy left nothing but suffering and chaos in its wake.

Over the course of more than a century during which the French crown claimed ownership of the gem, two kings died of diseases that left their bodies deformed, another king and a queen were executed by their people like common criminals, the institution of the monarchy itself collapsed, and an entire nation descended into financial ruin, starvation, war, and chaos.

The Diamond Resurfaces

In 1812, two decades after the French Blue disappeared without a trace, a large, fine, deep-blue diamond appeared in England. The London jeweler John Francillion described an extraordinary stone weighing roughly 45.5 carats, which was at the time in the possession of a diamond merchant named Daniel Elliason. This diamond, unlike the French Blue, was smaller and had a more conventional cut, known as a cushion. Considering how rare blue diamonds are, let alone as large, fine, and deep as this one, it was generally accepted that the stone described by Francillion and the fateful French Blue were one and the same, despite the diamonds' differences. Elliason later sold this gem to King George IV. If the diamond did indeed bear a curse, it seemed to have little effect in England.

Throughout his life, King George was maligned by the press for his "all-absorbing selfishness" and taste for luxury (which may have led him to purchase the French Blue in the first place). He died in 1830 without an heir and encumbered by enormous debts, which were so large that his estate sold the diamond to a private buyer. However, George died relatively peacefully at the age of sixty-three, having retired at Windsor Castle, and England, then at the cusp of the an economic boom spurred on by the Industrial Revolution, fared well during his reign.

It would be nine more years before the blue diamond was heard from again: this time, it would be under a new name. In 1839, a well-known and wealthy gem collector named Henry Philip Hope published a catalog of those precious stones in his possession. Among them was the very large deep-blue cushion-cut diamond. With the catalog's publication, one of the world's most famous gems had a new appearance and a new name: the Hope Diamond.

Evalyn Walsh McLean

After the publication of Hope's catalog, the Hope Diamond crisscrossed the Atlantic Ocean, changing hands all the while. Henry Philip Hope's grandson, Lord Francis Hope, inherited the stone and was forced to sell it due to financial troubles; it eventually passed to the New York City-based jewelers Joseph Frankel's Sons & Co., whose business was near ruin by the time they sold it to Selim Habib; Habib, in turn, met his own bad fate, at least according to a 1909 article in the *New York Times* that states:

> Habib Selim Habib, a wealthy Turkish diamond collector and merchant, who formerly owned the famous blue Hope Diamond, was among the passengers drowned in the wreck of the French mail steamer *Seyne* at Singapore. This adds another to the list of misfortunes associated with the ownership of the famous gem. It is reported that he had the diamond with him.

The fashionable heiress Evalyn Walsh McLean poses with the Hope Diamond.

The Hope Diamond, which, according to the *New York Times*, lay at the bottom of the sea, somehow made its way to the renowned French jeweler Pierre Cartier, who began looking for a buyer. By this point, rumors that the Hope Diamond was cursed had become popular, and Cartier was facing an uphill battle in selling it. In 1911, however, Cartier would find a buyer in an American socialite named Evalyn Walsh McLean.

McLean was born to Thomas Walsh, an Irish immigrant who became a multimillionaire after discovering a gold deposit outside Ouray, Colorado. McLean came of age in the lap of luxury, and she developed an appetite for jewels—as McLean herself said, "I cannot help it if I have a passion for jewels. The truth is, when I neglect to wear them, astute members of my family call in doctors!"

When McLean and her husband, Edward Beale McLean, whose family owned the *Washington Post*, visited Paris, Pierre Cartier jumped on the opportunity to make the sale of a lifetime. According to McLean's autobiography, Cartier, who had previously sold the heiress a $120,000 diamond named the Star of the East, visited the family in their hotel suite, where he delivered a tantalizing sales pitch: the blue diamond he had brought with him, he said, bore a curse that spelled ruin and death for all who possessed it (except, it seems, Cartier himself, who made a fortune building one of the world's most famous and lucrative luxury jewelry brands).

The pitch appealed to McLean's adventurous spirit, but the jewelry itself did not, so Cartier left the hotel empty-handed. He eventually returned with the stone now mounted on a circlet, which proved more appealing to McLean, but she still wasn't sold. Cartier encouraged her to take it home for a few days and think about it, so she placed it on her dresser. According to McLean, "For hours that jewel stared at me, and at some time during the night I began to really want the thing. Then I put the chain around my neck and hooked my life to its destiny for good or evil." The McLeans agreed to pay the $180,000 Cartier wanted for the cursed stone.

For some time, McLean lived the charmed life of a wealthy Washington heiress, attending parties and hosting guests at the family mansion on Massachusetts Avenue, always with the

Hope Diamond around her neck. McLean believed that the stone that seemed to have brought so much bad luck would in fact do the opposite for her, and she came to associate with the gem.

Unfortunately, McLean would not own the diamond without her fair share of tragedy. In 1919, McLean's firstborn son Vinson was struck and killed by a car outside the family home at the age of nine. McLean's husband Edward, perhaps to numb the pain of the loss of their son, began drinking heavily, took a mistress, and was later declared insane and committed to a psychiatric hospital where he died due to alcohol poisoning.

During this time, the *Washington Post* went bankrupt and McLean was forced to sell it. In 1946, McLean's only daughter, Evalyn McLean Reynolds, died of a drug overdose. McLean never recovered from the loss, and she died of pneumonia shortly after, in 1947. Her estate was so encumbered that her jewelry collection, including her cherished blue diamond, was sold.

National Treasure

New York City–based jeweler Harry Winston purchased the Hope Diamond from the McLean estate in 1949. For a little less than a decade, the Hope Diamond traveled the world alongside many other famous gems in Winston's "Court of Jewels" exhibit. In 1958, with the family having suffered no ill effects as a result of owning the stone, Winston donated the Hope Diamond to the Smithsonian in Washington, DC. An employee at Winston's jewelry store packaged the Hope Diamond in an ordinary box wrapped in brown paper and handed it off to the US Postal Service. The total cost of postage: $2.44. Winston also paid a little under $150 for the package to be insured for up to $1 million. The gem arrived safely at the Smithsonian's Natural History Museum on November 10, two days after it was mailed, and it has been the centerpiece of the Smithsonian's collection ever since.

The Final Victim

The donation of the Hope Diamond to the Smithsonian seems to have brought an end to the curse. According to the museum's curators, the stone may be bringing good luck as millions of visitors flock to get a look at it. However, many believe there was one more person who fell victim to the stone's curse.

Former police officer Paul Haase delivers a package containing the Hope Diamond to the post office.

On November 10, 1958, letter carrier James G. Todd picked up the package containing the Hope Diamond from the Washington, DC, city post office and delivered it to the Smithsonian. Within a year of the delivery, Todd was twice hit by a car, suffering a crushed leg and a head injury; his wife died of a heart attack; his dog was suffocated by its own leash; and a fire broke out in his house.

Despite all that happened to him, Todd later told the *Washington Post* that he did not believe in the curse. "Perhaps I'm actually having good luck," he said when speaking about the fire that partially destroyed his house. "Thank God all four children were outside instead of in those rooms."

Diamonds are beautiful and are closely associated with life's romantic moments, but there is no evidence proving that they are any more than stones.

Unraveling the Curse

C urses make for entertaining legends and instructive tales about what not to do, but there is usually little evidence to indicate that curses are responsible for people's misfortune. From the curse of the pharaohs to the curse of the Bambino, curses have been shown time and again to come up short in regards to scientific truth. Even the Hope Diamond, whose history is full of **anecdotal** evidence about financial ruin and death, seems to be just another priceless gem.

Fact and Fiction

Often, the only evidence that leads people to believe in a curse are stories that have been told over and over again. As a person relates the story behind a certain object that is supposedly cursed, there is a tendency to focus on the number of cases in which a person experiences misfortune as a result of coming into contact with the object. The greater the number of cases associated with the curse, the more likely it will seem that the curse is real.

The curse of the Bambino is a perfect example of how history seems to "favor" the belief in a certain hex. Every year that the Red Sox did not win a World Series championship after Ruth was traded seemed to pile on evidence. Five years without a World Series win seems suspicious, but *eighty years* made it seem like the team would never win again! However, what many people fail to realize is that lots of sports teams experience such droughts (but few for so long). In fact, eight baseball teams have never won a championship. The oldest of such teams, the Texas Rangers, which were founded in 1961, has gone fifty-five years without a championship win.

The curse of the pharaohs during Carter's expedition to find King Tut's tomb is another example. At the time of the discovery, many people focused on the fact that Carter's sponsor, Lord Carnarvon, died within months of stepping foot in the tomb, and that five others also died. Although that may seem like compelling evidence, people often forget to mention the details. For one, the six members of Carter's team who died were less than 25 percent of the total number of people who entered the tomb. Each of these people who died over the course of years had been living in crude conditions and performing hard labor digging through dirt and sand in an unforgiving desert environment. Each of these factors likely caused health problems or made existing problems, such as those which Lord Carnarvon was known to suffer, that much worse.

When people are selective about the details surrounding a legend like the curse of the pharaohs, it makes the legend seem much more believable than it is. However, details such as these give a more well-rounded picture and explain the cases of "misfortune" much more scientifically than a curse.

Reverse the Curse

Superstitions like curses also lead to superstitions about how to cure them. Many of these seem outlandish and even silly, but people who believe in a curse genuinely believe superstitions can help erase the effects of the curse. However, these often fail to have any effect.

Sports fans are among the most suspicious groups of people, and the most famous curse in sports—the curse of the Bambino—has given rise to a number of possible "solutions" over the decades. These have ranged from the practical, such as changing the "Reverse Curve" sign on Starrow Drive in Boston to "Reverse the Curse," to the mystical. Perhaps the most elaborate counter-curse surfaced in 2001, when Red Sox fan Paul Giorgio asked a Buddhist monk how the hex might be halted. Acting on the monk's recommendation, Giorgio, an avid mountain climber, went to the summit of Mount Everest, the tallest mountain in the world, and placed a Red Sox cap there. When he returned to base camp, Giorgio then burned a Yankees cap. Despite the great lengths (and extraordinary height) he had gone to cancel the curse, it would still be three more years before the Red Sox would win a championship.

The "final" cure for the curse of the Bambino, at least according to many sports fans, came in 2004 as the result of a fluke. In July, Red Sox player Manny Ramirez hit a foul ball that flew into the stands. The ball hit a young boy, knocking out two of his teeth. The boy, it was later discovered, lived in the same house that Babe Ruth—the Bambino—once owned. That year, the Red Sox won their first World Series since trading Babe Ruth.

How are these sorts of solutions meant to work, however? Just like the curses they are meant to counteract, such measures more often than not do nothing at all. When they do finally "work" and the curse is "lifted," the exact method seems convoluted and nonsensical. In the case of the curse of the Bambino, besides the connection between the young fan who was accidentally struck and Babe Ruth, there is nothing to indicate why the accident would finally end the curse. Babe Ruth was long dead, and if he was alive and if he did hold enough animosity toward his former team for trading him, why would he care that a fan had lost a couple of teeth? Just as with curses, the cures seem equally as farfetched.

A Closer Look at the Hope Diamond

There are few allegedly cursed objects that have as long or as rich a history as the Hope Diamond—after all, it's been around for about a billion years. From the royal courts of French kings to the stately mansion of an American heiress, the Hope Diamond has changed hands dozens of times. All of that history has given the jinxed jewel plenty of time to be associated with some of the worst tragedies of the past. However, does the number of stories mean that the Hope Diamond is, in fact, cursed? The answer, it seems, is no.

First of all, not every owner of the Hope Diamond has fallen victim to a "curse." Jean-Baptiste Tavernier, who was the first European to own what would become the Hope Diamond, was a successful merchant who accumulated wealth and status during his lifetime. Although little is known about how he died, it seems likely that he passed away in relative comfort. Additionally, the man from whom the Hope Diamond gets its name, Henry Phillip Hope, was also wealthy, amassing an impressive collection of rare and historically significant jewels, and seemed to escape any consequence of the curse. The stone's latest owner, the Smithsonian Institution, has publicly stated that the curse has been overblown, instead arguing that their prize exhibit has been a source of good luck for the museum since its donation in 1958.

Someone who believes in the Hope Diamond's curse might argue that the fact that the Hope Diamond hasn't affected all of its owners the same way doesn't necessarily mean it isn't cursed. It is possible that it might just cause more harm to certain people over others. What about those few individuals who befell tragedy during their period of ownership?

The argument against the belief that cursed objects are to blame for people's misfortunes is perhaps best summarized by an owner who had lost so much. In her autobiography, Evalyn

Walsh McLean, who withstood probably the greatest number of losses during her ownership of the Hope Diamond, said, "What tragedies have befallen me might have occurred had I never seen or touched the Hope Diamond. My observations have persuaded me that tragedies, for anyone who lives, are not escapable."

A LIKELY STORY

Another contributing factor to the widespread belief in curses involves the way stories about the curse are reported in the media. Newspapers, magazines, and books want to inform their readers, but they also want to make money, and more sensationalist stories are more likely to sell more copies. Once one type of story begins to catch on, other sources of media might also begin reporting the same story, making it seem like the story is truer.

The curse of the pharaohs is a perfect example of this back-and-forth in the media. According to Egyptologist Dominic Montserrat, Carter's discovery of King Tut's tomb was not the first mention of a curse. During the nineteenth century, many theaters in London, England, offered macabre shows in which a mummy recovered from Egypt was stripped of its burial wrappings in front of a crowd. Eventually, authors who were possibly entranced or disgusted (or both) by the display began writing stories about a "Mummy's Curse" in which the disrobed corpse comes back to life to seek vengeance on those who humiliated it. When the media got word of Carter's real-life discovery, many began reporting it alongside these fictional stories.

Indiana Jones may have crisscrossed the world to protect cursed objects, but it seems curses don't exist outside of the silver screen.

CHAPTER FIVE

Closing the Case on Curses

The myth of the mummy, the Bambino, the Hope Diamond—these and other curses have been the subjects of countless articles, books, plays, feature films, and songs. Movie audiences have marveled at the vengeance of a mummy whose eternal rest has been disturbed, or rode across the desert with daring archaeologists on missions to protect a dazzling artifact. However, it is important to keep in mind that the real-life inspirations for these larger-than-life blockbusters are far less romantic and far more complicated.

Kicking the Curse

There is no scientific reason to believe that anything is cursed. A cursed object is just a thing, an inanimate material possession. History shows that the objects that are allegedly cursed, such as King Tut's tomb or the Hope Diamond, do not seem to have any effect because they do not "affect" people at all. Those people who have encountered certain items and then experienced tragedy would have likely had the same experiences if they had never encountered the thing at all.

What is it then about curses that people continue to return to time after time? Maybe the answer lies in the human attraction to a good story. Many legends about cursed objects often involve things that people love to hear about. In the case of the Hope Diamond, it is a legend almost as old as time, full of globetrotting merchants exploring the farthest corners of the world, kings wrapped up in the management of their courts, a murdered queen, wealthy heirs and tycoons, and even the collapse of a nation. It is a story about fortunes made and lost, about power and desire, about wealth and vengeance. And at the center of it all, a curious blue diamond, forged deep in the earth, cut to a beautiful brilliance. Through all of the intrigue, the financial ruin, the death, the Hope Diamond remains, as silent as a stone.

The Hope Diamond will forever entrance those who view it.

TO HAVE AND TO HOLD

Although evidence for the existence of curses cannot be scientifically proven, and many of the stories about these possessions have been embellished over the course of the centuries that they have been told, legends of misfortune, illness, death, and murder continue to swirl around cursed objects. Why? What about these things captivate people? What about them sparks this curious combination of apprehension and curiosity?

Perhaps the reason for our fear of these so-called cursed objects is because they are both things to avoid as well as things we want: a priceless diamond, the untold riches of a sealed-off tomb, the land in a new country. Maybe the real "curse" of these objects is in our desire to possess them. They are cautionary tales we tell one another and ourselves to be wary of wanting too much—that in possessing a thing, the thing might come to possess us.

GLOSSARY

anecdotal Based on the word of outside observers.

carat A unit of weight for precious stones.

crown jewel The jewels, especially the crown and scepter, worn by a monarch.

crust The outermost layer of Earth's geology, characterized by cool, solid rock.

curse A wish, prayer, spell, or other evil energy meant to cause harm or misfortune to a person or people.

cut The shape of a diamond.

igneous A type of rock formed from hardened magma.

mantle The largest part of Earth's geology between the core and the crust, characterized by mostly hot, molten rock.

supernatural Describing something existing outside of the observable universe.

superstition A belief or practice stemming from a widely held but unjustified idea that one thing causes another.

taboo Something that is forbidden based on morality.

tectonic plate One of several huge sub-layers of crust that move and sometimes collide into another.

trope A commonly used literary device, such as a metaphor or theme.

FURTHER INFORMATION

Books

Harrison, Paul. *The Curse of the Pharaohs' Tombs: Tales of the Unexpected Since the Days of Tutankhamun.* Barnsley, UK: Pen and Sword, 2017.

Hawass, Zahi. *The Curse of the Pharaohs: My Adventures with Mummies.* Washington, DC: National Geographic Society, 2004.

Kurin, Richard. *The Hope Diamond: The Legendary History of a Cursed Gem.* New York: HarperCollins, 2007.

Shaughnessy, Dan. *The Curse of the Bambino.* New York: Penguin Books, 2004.

Websites

Encyclopedia Smithsonian: The Hope Diamond
http://www.si.edu/Encyclopedia_SI/nmnh/hope.htm
This site, hosted by the Smithsonian Institute, features a brief historical overview, quick facts about the diamond, and links to further information.

Mental Floss: 10 Allegedly Cursed Objects Throughout History
http://mentalfloss.com/article/59504/10-allegedly-cursed-objects-throughout-history
Mental Floss offers this catalog of legendary objects.

National Geographic: The Curse of the Mummy
http://science.nationalgeographic.com/science/archaeology/curse-of-the-mummy
Read about the history behind the curse of the pharaohs as well as the field of Egyptology.

Videos

National Geographic: King Tut's Curse
http://www.nationalgeographic.com.au/videos/egypt/king-tuts-curse-part-1-1002.aspx
Follow in the footsteps of Howard Carter and explore the mysteries contained within King Tut's tomb for yourself … if you dare.

Smithsonian Channel: Mystery of the Hope Diamond
http://www.smithsonianchannel.com/shows/mystery-of-the-hope-diamond/0/136360
This documentary, hosted by the Smithsonian Institution, is the next best thing to visiting the actual Hope Diamond in Washington, DC.

BIBLIOGRAPHY

"Curse of the Hope Diamond: The Misfortunes of Evalyn Walsh McLean." Smithsonian Museum of Natural Sciences. 2016. Accessed December 13, 2016. http://mineralsciences.si.edu/collections/hope/details/the-misfortunes-of-evalyn-walsh-mclean.htm.

Evers, Jeanine, ed. "Mantle." *National Geographic.* Accessed December 6, 2016. http://nationalgeographic.org/encyclopedia/mantle.

"The Four Layers." *Volcano World.* Oregon State University. Accessed December 6, 2016. http://volcano.oregonstate.edu/earths-layers-lesson-1.

Gates, Henry Leyford. *The Mystery of the Hope Diamond.* New York: International Copyright Bureau, 1921.

"The Great Explorer and Merchant Jean-Baptiste Tavernier." Smithsonian Museum of Natural Sciences. 2016. Accessed December 11, 2016. http://mineralsciences.si.edu/collections/hope/details/jean-baptiste-tavernier.htm.

Handwerk, Brian. "Curse of the Mummy." *National Geographic.* Accessed December 29, 2016. http://science.nationalgeographic.com/science/archaeology/curse-of-the-mummy.

"Hope Diamond: Timeline." PBS. Accessed December 13, 2016. http://www.pbs.org/treasuresoftheworld/hope/ hlevel_1/htimeline.html.

Latson, Jennifer. "The Origins of the 'Pharaoh's Curse' Legend." *Time*. November 26, 2014. http://time.com/3594676/king-tut.

Lineberry, Cate. "Diamonds Unearthed." *Smithsonian Magazine*. December 2006. http://www.smithsonianmag. com/science-nature/diamonds-unearthed-141629226.

"Louis XV (1710-1774)." BBC. 2014. http://www.bbc.co.uk/ history/historic_figures/louis_xv.shtml.

"Louis XVI." Chateau Versailles. Accessed December 13, 2016. http://en.chateauversailles.fr/history/court-people/ louis-xvi-time/louis-xvi.

Parissien, Dr. Steven. "George IV: The Royal Joke?" BBC. February 17, 2011. http://www.bbc.co.uk/history/british/ empire_seapower/george_fourth_01.shtml.

Platon, Mircea. "Storming the Bastille (July 14, 1789)." Ohio State University. July 2014. http://origins.osu.edu/ milestones/july-2014-storming-bastille.

Pope, Nancy. "Delivering the Hope Diamond." Smithsonian's National Postal Museum Blog. November 11, 2008. http://postalmuseumblog.si.edu/2012/11/delivering-the-hope-diamond.html.

Schultz, Colin. "How Do We Know the Earth is 4.6 Billion Years Old?" Smithsonian. May 16, 2014. Accessed December 6, 2016. http://www.smithsonianmag.com/smart-news/how-do-we-know-earth-46-billion-years-old-180951483.

Surugue, Léa. "Tomb in Giza Pyramid is protected by a 'primitive machine' built by the ancient Egyptians." *International Business Times*. July 13, 2016. http://www.ibtimes.co.uk/subbed-ancient-egyptians-protected-their-pharaohs-tombs-primitive-machine-1570464.

Tavernier, Jean-Baptiste. *Travels in India*. New York: MacMillan and Co., 1889. https://archive.org/details/travelsinindia00tavegoog.

"Treasures of the World: The Notorious Hope Diamond." PBS. Accessed December 14, 2016. http://www.pbs.org/treasuresoftheworld/a_nav/hope_nav/main_hopfrm.html.

Wise, Richard W. "Tavernier, Later Travels & Peter the Great." The French Blue. 2010. http://www.thefrenchblue.com/article2.htm#.

INDEX

ABOUT THE AUTHOR

Andrew Coddington has written a number of books for Cavendish Square on a wide variety of topics, including history and the paranormal. In addition to *The Hope Diamond, Cursed Objects, and Unexplained Artifacts*, he has written *The Bermuda Triangle, Stonehenge, and Unexplained Places* and *Aliens, UFOs, and Unexplained Encounters* in the Paranormal Investigations series. He lives in Buffalo, New York, with his wife and dog.